# <u>HOW TO PROPERLY INSULT A DEMOCRAT</u>

### <u>Voting Guide for Gen X,Y,Z, Millennials and Boomers.</u>

*"I cannot and will not recant anything, for to go against conscience is neither right nor safe. Here I stand, I can do no other, so help me God. Amen."* Martin Luther April 18, 1521

- If you don't understand our country is brand new and still working out the bugs, vote Democrat.

- If you want to kill babies, vote Democrat.

- **If Trans Female and want everyone to believe your balls are just low-hanging ovaries, vote Democrat.**

- **If you want the 2020 census to resemble taking attendance in first grade, vote Democrat. Is Joey here? No, he's in the bathroom. Oh, OK.**

- **If Black or Hispanic and hypnotized by Democrats to vote for candidates who continue destroying your neighborhood, vote Democrat.**

- **If you support Slavery, vote Democrat because illegal immigration is a form of Slavery. (Coyote Debt and Sex Slavery)**

- If able to produce bald-faced lies without remorse, vote Democrat. It's a skill that takes years to develop so just be sure to train your kids early.

- If rat souffle should be on the menu in all Democrat-run metrosexual hot spots, vote Democrat.

- Listen up GenX/Millennials: If "entitled, disengaged, lazy and hard to manage"(sic) vote Democrat, but should you change party affiliation those attributes will improve over time.

- If most American jobs should be eliminated to make way for a welfare state, vote Democrat.

- If American women should wear Hijabs, vote Democrat.

• If post-term abortion seems appropriate, vote Democrat then consider aborting yourself since it's safe, legal and rare.

• If you can't recognize nor admit Global Warming is a Blessing, vote Democrat. (Outer Space is 450 friggin' degrees below zero!) And you want to make the Earth colder? Are you kidding me? Google it.

• While living in Baltimore, Detroit, Chicago, San Francisco or L.A and wish to declare asylum in Guatemala, vote Democrat.

• If willing to donate your citizenship to an illegal alien, vote Democrat, then self-deport.

● **If you support the Congressional Meesohorny Sexual Escapade Fund, vote Democrat. It's the 'patriotic' thing to do.**

● **If able to explain why sky-high murder rates are exclusively seen in gun-controlled Liberal cities, vote Democrat.**

● **If Arabic should be mandatory in all primary and secondary schools, vote Democrat.**

● **If we should offer in-utero gender transitioning to every child born in America, vote Democrat.**

● **If born between 1619-1865, enslaved, and alive, you definitely deserve reparations, so vote Democrat. But if all the above criteria are not met, STFU.**

• If 'Deliverance' is your perceived image of America, vote Democrat.

• Listen carefully GenX/Millennials: Capitalism makes you richer and Socialism poorer. If that's not patently obvious, vote Democrat, then getcha some book learnin'.

• If male using Men's Rooms or female using Woman's Rooms, vote Democrat but that's sexist. Unisex Diapers? Problem solved.

• If all demented nursing home residents should be forced to testify before Congress, vote Democrat. Those little day trips seem to help.

- **If killing female babies is now a feminist position, vote Democrat.**

- **To GenX/Millennials: Since American Colleges offer the equivalent of a 3rd-grade education, vote Democrat. PS: HS grads come out with a 1st-grade education which doesn't help.**

- **If White Supremacy is the same as White Majority, vote Democrat.**

- **If the Taliban should be our 'Third Party", vote Democrat.**

- **Since you believe in the Global Warming Doomsday Clock, vote Democrat, then board the first spaceship to**

Mars which is considerably cooler and offers limitless opportunities for real estate development.


• If all bakeries should be forced to bake whatever anyone demands whether they like it or not, vote Democrat.


• If men and women are exactly the same, vote Democrat. But, then why is everyone transitioning?


• Listen carefully GenX/Millennials: If you don't understand the more CO2 we pump into the atmosphere the GREENER our planet, vote Democrat. PS: Compare satellite images from 50 years ago to today. The difference will astound you.

• If sharing your home with let's say… a dozen illegal aliens seems like the best solution to our immigration problem, vote Democrat.

• If you just can't wait to watch beheadings on Sunday afternoon instead of the NFL, vote Democrat.

• If you can convincingly explain why Hawaii should remain a State and Puerto Rico a territory, vote Democrat. At least Alaska has oil. We can park our damn boats somewhere else.

• If you walk around with a chip on your shoulder, vote Democrat. Now I'm not talking about "The Squad" here. No way.

• If 'participation awards' should be offered for daily colon evacuation, vote Democrat. " Now presenting the Brown Medal Award..."

• If seeing millions of birds get chopped up in wind farms is something you can really get behind, vote Democrat, and please notify nearby restaurants in case they run low on their 'daily specials'.

• Listen up GenX/Millennials: Since America is among the worst countries for women, vote Democrat. That's right, death by stoning, forced marriages, female infanticide, sex slavery, and domestic servitude are all rampant right here in the good old USA. "Safety first", so I recommend all American women move to Iran or Saudi Arabia. Conjugal visits to be arranged at a later date if the women haven't already been stoned to death.

● **If you forget that America is set up where 'ya gotta work ta get stuff, vote Democrat.**

● **If all hamburgers should be made exclusively from the stuff you get outta your vacuum cleaner bag, vote Democrat.**

● **If guns are more dangerous than people, vote Democrat.**

● **If you are an ungrateful self-centered egotistical purple-haired lesbian bitch who won't go to the White House after having the honor of representing your country, vote Democrat.**

• Whereas all life on Earth will soon disappear in a Global Warming Catastrophe, vote Democrat, but wouldn't it be better to just stay home in air-conditioned comfort and let others vote since you'll be dead soon anyway?

• If you're a blood-sucking freeloader posing as a Democrat representative, vote Democrat then call "Trump Pest Control".

• "If you Hate your Doctor you can keep your Doctor", seems like Obamacare is working, vote Democrat.

• Listen up GenX/Millennials: If you think Green energy is cleaner than fossil-based, vote Democrat. It's not. Why? Because mining rare earth minerals, silver, nickel, aluminum, cobalt, and lithium leave the Earth devastated all the while employing slave labor exposing them to levels of toxic waste rarely seen in human history. Why do you think we moved it to China?

● If recently elected Muslim representatives should try and convert all Americans to Islam, vote Democrat. She said it, not me.

● If affirmative action makes any sense whatsoever, vote Democrat, then look at your boss.

● If the phrase "In God We Trust" triggers an uncontrollable emotional response, vote Democrat, then send me all your cash so we can help ease your suffering.

• If women should be the only ones to bear children, vote Democrat, but that's sexist and reeks of discrimination.

• If you hate America, vote Democrat, but eventually you may find the country hates you back.

• If "Somebody did something on 9/11" effects no outrage, vote Democrat.

• Listen up GenX/Millennials: Believing in Toxic Masculinity, vote Democrat, then take off your makeup, high heels, tight low cut dress, push up bra, nail polish, perfume, and jewelry. Women rule this country in myriad ways. Did I forget Plastic Surgery and Botox?

• If Woke, vote Democrat but that's just Political Correctness with veiled Racism.

• If intersectionality is your thing, vote Democrat; but you better be an Uneducated Disabled Poor Foreign-born Black Lesbian Muslim Woman. Otherwise, STFU.

• If you support Education Reparations (student debt relief), vote Democrat but you must also send reparations to students who worked 2-3 part-time jobs and owe nothing, those who have already paid off their loans and those who couldn't afford college in the first place.

• If Jihad is worship, vote Democrat.

• If gas should be $7/gallon as in Europe, vote Democrat. Have you seen European cars lately?

• If smiling, hugging or putting your kids to bed is sexual abuse, vote Democrat.

• To GenX/Millennials: If Black or Brown and don't understand you are as integral as Whites to the running of this country, vote Democrat. Oops, did I suggest 'all lives matter'?

• If you wanna be suicidal and depressed immediately after Trump wins, vote Democrat.

• Listen up GenX/Millennials: If calling countries S***holes offends your sensibility, vote Democrat, but most Democrat-controlled cities are S***holes and you do nothing to fix them except re-elect Democrats.

- If Faith, Family, Tradition, and Heritage are old fashioned, vote Democrat.

- To GenX/Millennials: Having been exclusively taught revisionist history and historical fiction since grade school, vote Democrat. The Soviets, Nazis, and Maoists did it. See where they ended up?

- If you're dumb enough to want electric cars without dotting the country with Nuclear Power Plants, vote Democrat.

- If the minimum wage should be slightly less than your I.Q., vote Democrat.

• **If you just won the Women's World Cup Soccer, vote Democrat, then burn your flag, get drunk, grab your crotch, finger yourself in public, go potty-mouth, and demand more money even though nobody really gives a crap about your sport.**

• **If you are White and believe all White People are disgusting, vote Democrat though self-reflection may be in order.**

• **Listen up GenX/Millennials: Since European cities are running out of blood due to migrant stabbing epidemics, vote Democrat. And you're worried about gun control?**

• If One Party Rule benefits American cities in any way, vote Democrat.

• If not understanding that except for the UK and its ex-colonies, America has no true friends or allies, vote Democrat. Trump understands this and governs accordingly. Obama? No clue. Bush and Clinton? Not really.

• If Diversity means skin color, vote Democrat, but doesn't that seem a bit restrictive?

• If 'men' or 'man' should be struck from the English language and replaced by 'youze people', vote Democrat.

• If you live in a S***hole while your representatives live in huge Mansions inside Heavily Walled Privately Secured Fully Gated Suburban Communities, vote Democrat.

• If telling the difference between Vermin and your elected officials is challenging, vote Democrat.

• If wanting to remove 'four zeros" from our currency just like Iran, vote Democrat. That's right, a Benjamin will be worth one cent.

• If you believe in free speech but hate when others disagree with you, vote Democrat.

• Listen up GenX/Millennials: The term "Health care" is nebulous so let's get more specific. If major surgery is ever needed, ( auto accident, work accident, cancer, violence, major trauma) surgical access and post-op care in America is unrivaled. Period. Wanna bleed to death? Vote Democrat.

- If reality is no longer fundamental, vote Democrat.

- If America should be run by Con Men and Pimps, vote Democrat.

- If 1% growth trumps 3% growth, vote Democrat. I know, you're just tired of winning.

- If rolling blackouts are fun for you and your family, vote Democrat.

• If routinely inviting prostitutes to pee on your bed, vote Democrat, 'cause Trump didn't and never will.

• If straight Americans should be called "non-LGBTQ", vote Democrat. The term 'straight' is so yesterday.

• Since most colleges and universities are now "Concentration Camps", vote Democrat, so Fascist Indoctrination Policies can be pursued with the vigor they so richly deserve.

• If you don't recognize Medicare for All means Health Care for None, vote Democrat.

• If you're too dumb to see that Trump doesn't care one bit about race, vote Democrat. It's all about

America. And besides, a racist NYC real estate developer? Bankrupt inside a year.

• Listen up GenX/Millennials: If you want to be the first generation to lose your right to privacy, vote Democrat. Oops, you have already.

• If you can go outside and not see that your neighborhood has never been greener, vote Democrat. Do it. You'll see. It's the CO2 'ya moron.

• Since all rich Republicans are out to screw you, vote Democrat. The rich Democrats? Well, they're all politicians screwing you behind your back.

• If 'values' have no value, vote Democrat.

- Since Trump is worse than Hitler/Stalin/Mao all put together, vote Democrat, but just so we're clear, roughly 100,000,000 people died at their hands. Trump? Fewer.

- If Hollywood Stars should run for President, vote Democrat. Can anybody really stand looking at those fools anymore?

- If you've finally elevated lying to an art form, vote Democrat.

- If Israel should disappear like Lex Luthor's brilliant plan to develop Costa del Lex, vote Democrat.

● If taking a knee makes you a hero, vote Democrat but real heroes may eventually have something to say about that.


● If the moon landing was "fake news", vote Democrat.


● If losing an election in Georgia means you just won an election in Georgia, vote Democrat. Hopefully, this will be the blueprint for all future elections.


● To GenX/Millennials: If you want to impede the 4th Industrial Revolution by taxing businesses to death and discouraging innovation, vote Democrat.


● If the ban on plastic straws simply stirs emotions in you that you barely thought possible, vote Democrat, because that's the most important issue this country faces and a known existential threat.

• If hateful rhetoric stirs you, vote Democrat.

• If Trump sounds like an idiot, vote Democrat, then listen to Jerry Nadler. The winner? Fat Jerry.

• If most other countries aren't S***holes, vote Democrat, but why is everyone trying to break in?

• If you prefer, "Made in China", vote Democrat, but China will ultimately impoverish the US if someone other than Trump is elected.

• If extremely gullible, vote Democrat. Now that doesn't mean your stupid or anything like that.

- **To GenX/Millennials: If you think Multiculturalism works, vote Democrat. It doesn't. Never has, and occasionally ends in full-blown civil war.**

- **Since Universities claim the words 'America' or 'American' is hate speech, vote Democrat so we can start book burning and crucifixion.**

- **If you can't recognize a heat-wave is just a heat-wave and not Global Warming, vote Democrat. I don't give a damn if it's >100 degrees out, that's not Global Warming. It's just hot where you are right now. Jeez.**

- **If The Deep State should run the country, vote Democrat. Oh wait, they do.**

• If Thought Police is your favorite law enforcement agency, vote Democrat.


• When you hear 'Socialism' and forget that it means 'Socialist Economy', vote Democrat. Listen carefully GenX/Millennials; a Socialist Economy will be an unmitigated disaster for you and your family. Socialist countries barely have electricity. Open your eyes.


• If your elected officials should accept money from mobs, racists, gangs, cartels and pedophiles, vote Democrat.


• If today's sports figures are role models, vote Democrat. They used to be. Well, maybe not OJ.

• **Listen up GenX/Millennials: If all symbols of past oppression should be removed, vote Democrat, but how are we supposed to remember what we shouldn't have been doing in the first place?**

• **If you want Obama on the $1,$2,$5,$10,$20,$50,$100,$500,$1000, $5000,$10,000 and $100,000 bill, vote Democrat. Many are out of print but don't worry, we'll just paste his picture on top of the old ones.**

• **If paranoid, vote Democrat because what party is out there keeping you safe at night? Democrats? Think again.**

• **If you have no idea how and why the Electoral College was set up, vote Democrat.**

● **Listen up GenX/Millennials: The Green New Deal and Medicare for All will gut our Military and you will be nuked, so if that's OK, vote Democrat. That's real 'Russian interference'.**

● **If hatred is your only emotion, vote Democrat.**

● **If throwing people in front of speeding trains by African migrants is a good source of recreation for our newly arrived friends, vote Democrat.**

● **If narratives are more important than truth, vote Democrat.**

• If you want Michael Avenatti to run for President, vote Democrat. Maybe he'll run while in prison? Doesn't matter, he's an excellent candidate.

• If you want your life to have limited meaning or no purpose whatsoever, vote Democrat.

• If you think your skin color disadvantages you, vote Democrat, then talk to shortfatuglywhite people.

• Listen up GenX/Millennials: You were born into the richest most freedom-loving country in the world and should make the most of it, but if that's not enough, vote Democrat.

• If call-centers should remain offshore, vote Democrat, then memorize the phrase "Can you repeat that please".

• If the Rio Grande should be overflowing with the bloated bodies of dead babies, vote Democrat.

• If bartenders should make our laws, vote Democrat.

• If unable to see the UN is useless and should be replaced by a 50 story Chick-fil-A, vote Democrat.

• If holding people accountable for destroying our Country is Racist, vote Democrat.

• If the history of this country is unknown to you, vote Democrat.

- If throwing eggs at Conservatives trying to engage in conversation is now considered a sport, vote Democrat.

- If toilet paper should be a luxury item like in Venezuela, vote Democrat.

- If you have a closet full of multi-colored tin foil hats, vote Democrat.

- If a Domestic Terrorist, vote Democrat.

- If you want to punch Trump in the face, vote Democrat, but he could probably beat the crap out of you.

- If Coastal Elites should occupy all college seats, vote Democrat.

- If you change your Gender Fluid as often as you change your motor oil, vote Democrat.

- If endlessly chanting the same rhyming phrase over and over again brings new insight focusing on problem-solving solutions, vote Democrat. Plus, you really look super smart.

- If an unmitigated Liberal-leaning non-stop freak show would be thoroughly entertaining for both you and your family, vote Democrat.

- If you think a higher minimum wage will increase productivity, vote Democrat.

- To GenX/Millennials: If you think your elected officials should look and sound exactly like you, vote Democrat, but you'll be disappointed.

- If you concede there are more genders than your SAT score, vote Democrat.

- If we need rampant European drug-resistant Syphilis coming here, vote Democrat. Gee, I wonder how it got there?

- If you believe in blocking hate speech, vote Democrat, but then who would you talk to?

- If you believe yourself to be totally incompetent, vote Democrat.

- If unemployed, vote Democrat because you're never going to work again.

- If licking or spitting on food is harmless fun, vote Democrat.

- If you want to be governed by a squad of Four White-hating angry bitches, vote Democrat.

- If death threats against Conservatives seem like a good way to motivate them, vote Democrat.

- Listen up Snowflakes: If all people should be selfless, loving and kind, vote Democrat, but I have to ask why we had to build all those nasty prisons?

- If you refuse to admit that Humans Self Segregate, vote Democrat. But if you open your eyes and recognize Self-Segregation is NOT racist, you may improve your understanding of Human Nature.

- If you think more of celebrities than you do of yourself, vote Democrat.

- If violence is the best way to solve our Nation's problems, vote Democrat.

- If you can't see Health Care is not a 'right' unless it's spelled out in the Constitution, vote Democrat. GenX/Millennials: the Fourth Industrial Revolution will transform Health Care so just be patient.

• If you forget without Military or Police you'd be speaking Russian or dead, vote Democrat.

• If Hollywood movies should be less entertaining and more preachy, vote Democrat.

• If you believe juvenile holding facilities on the Southern Border are run like kennels, vote Democrat. If you visit, bring lots of Puppy Chow.

• To GenX/Millennials: If you want to be the first generation to be hacked to death by MS-13, vote Democrat, but machetes aren't guns so you have nothing to worry about.

• If you think Groupthink is thinking, vote Democrat.

• **If you want to request Asylum in Mexico, vote Democrat.**

• **If you have no intention of taking advantage of the boundless opportunities afforded to all American citizens, vote Democrat.**

• **To GenX/Millennials: If you don't understand that Socialist policies and unbridled Illegal Immigration are why you are struggling, vote Democrat.**

• **If you honestly believe your elected officials will shower you with love, vote Democrat. They actually say that. Seriously. The reality is most Democrat lawmakers find you beneath contempt with few if any redeeming qualities.**

• If you want Obama back, vote Democrat, but that's obviously racist, and sexist too because he frequently identifies as a man.

• If you want to plant more trees, vote Democrat; that will lower CO2 levels which will lower food production and people will starve to death but at least you'll feel better.

• If the assassination of Republicans is exactly what they deserve, vote Democrat.

• If Demagoguery is always the best strategy, vote Democrat.

• If you love rioting, wearing black masks and beating the crap out of people, vote Democrat.

- If "One Nation Under God" should be replaced by "One Planet Under A Global Centralized Control", vote Democrat.

- If censorship is 'tough love', vote Democrat.

- If you're white then you're a racist, so vote Democrat because the country wasn't racist until Trump became President.

- If you want dumber kids, vote Democrat.

- If free speech and freedom of thought are no longer considered American ideals, vote Democrat.

• If you believe Michelle Obama is really the most admired woman in the world, vote Democrat, though many people hate her for being so Anti-American, arrogant and racist, but she would make a super-great President.

• To GenX/Millennials: If you have no problem with open borders and unlimited Green Cards, vote Democrat: Then apply for welfare.

• If insecure enough to watch CNN or MSNBC, vote Democrat.

• If you don't recognize civilian gun ownership and civilian-military oversight are unique to our country, vote Democrat.

- If you love RINOs, vote Democrat, 'cause you're in the same party.

- Listen carefully GenX/Millennials: If you forget Climate Change is measured in thousands or millions of years, vote Democrat. Please repeat that to yourselves until you actually don't forget.

- If Independence Day should be replaced by 'Too bad England didn't wipe our Ass Day', vote Democrat.

- If Anti-American rhetoric moves you, vote Democrat.

- If you honestly know what the Democrat party stands for, vote Democrat. You don't. Nobody does.

- If Maxine Waters and Fredericka Wilson are 'class acts', vote Democrat.

- If you believe "When they go low, we go lower and lower and lower still, vote Democrat.

- If you don't understand that WWIII will last about 15 min and be totally Cyber, vote Democrat. To GenX/Millennials: We build up our Military so nobody will dare launch a nuclear attack and vaporize you.

- If the ends always justify the means, vote Democrat.

- If Whites should all be sent back to Europe, vote Democrat.

● If representatives should run on a single issue like Global Warming, vote Democrat because this country has only one issue to resolve.

● If you would like everybody from Mexico, Central, and South America to have dual American citizenship, vote Democrat.

● If you are a Russian spy, vote Democrat because that party is the closest thing you've got to Mother Russia.

● If afraid of Blexit, and you should be, vote Democrat, but you're probably a racist.

● To GenX/Millennials: If you spend and budget your money like the Government, vote Democrat. The real question now is who will go belly-up first? You will.

• If you prefer name-calling to policy debate, vote Democrat.

• If every TV series and Movie should exclusively feature gay characters, vote Democrat. Oh wait, they do.

• If you belong to Antifa, vote Democrat.

• If you want to encourage overwhelming personal debt and drug abuse, vote Democrat.

• If your political ideas come from Glamour Magazines, vote Democrat.

• If Washington DC should be renamed Putinville, vote Democrat. Maybe Russia won't interfere in our elections quite as much. As if they did.

• If AOC is simply brilliant, vote Democrat, but that just might mean you're retarded.

• Listen up GenX/Millennials: If embarrassed when traveling outside the U.S. because you're American, vote Democrat. Republicans know they're just a bunch of jealous SOB's.

• If Donald Trump has untreated Central Nervous System Syphilis, vote Democrat. He may but I'd still vote for him.

- Since Impeachment is the only advisable thing to do, vote Democrat. I dare you. No, I double dare you.

- If you want to live in a cave to save the environment, vote Democrat.

- If you never tire of listening to the same talking points, vote Democrat.

- If comfortable with food thrown at White Conservatives out to dinner, vote Democrat.

- If you want to marry your brother, vote Democrat.

- If rapists, arsonists, serial killers, and pedophiles should be able to vote in our elections for a 'better society', vote Democrat.

- If it's OK for TransFemales to trounce CisFemales in Weightlifting Championships, vote Democrat. Say goodbye to that sport forever.

- If White people should apologize to every non-White person they meet, vote Democrat.

- If you've got a real hankerin' for a full-blown race war, vote Democrat.

- To GenX/Millennials: If you think money is the root of all evil, vote Democrat. Republicans know it's just a tool to evaluate value and risk.

- If the country should be run by Lobbyists and Special Interests, vote Democrat.

• **The Earth spins at 1000MPH, circles the sun at 67,000MPH, circles our galaxy at 515,000MPH and our galaxy moves through the Universe at 1,300,000MPH and you think we can predict Climate? If you do, vote Democrat. We can't even predict weather more than 5 days out. On top of that, the Universe is expanding at 153,000MPH and you think Climate Science is real?**

• **If the Bill of Rights has no meaning for you, vote Democrat.**

• **Listen up GenX/Millennials: If you think Universal Basic Income 'creates jobs', vote Democrat. It's been tried before. It doesn't. It will destroy you and your** family. Read about " U.S. negative income tax experiments".

• If you only speak English and feel embarrassed, vote Democrat.

• If you hate the American Experiment, vote Democrat. "American Exceptionalism", to me, sounds a bit arrogant.

• If you are high all the time, vote Democrat.

• If you want College dorms, Professor's homes, Hollywood mansions and Coastal elite to house illegal aliens, vote Democrat.

• If you want your ex-President to be too self-important to meet our adversaries, vote Democrat.

• To GenX/Millennials: If work culture is more important than your salary, vote Democrat, but you'll never own anything and retire impoverished at age 150.

• If you love social media platforms, vote Democrat. Today Conservative thought is censored, tomorrow it's you.

• If you like the whole notion of 'European Royalty', vote Democrat.

• If private property is unfairly distributed and racist, vote Democrat, then donate all your stuff to a Poor White Conservative. Feel better?

• **If you want America to be more dependent on other countries, vote Democrat.**

• **If anxious for Immigration-related Municipal bankruptcies, vote Democrat. They sure have done wonders for Europe.**

• **If Angel Moms should just shut-the-hell-up and get over it, vote Democrat.**

• **If you are Woke enough to still be using Gillette Blades, vote Democrat.**

• **If living in a tent on a filthy inner-city street is something to which you aspire, vote Democrat.**

- **If you majored in Victimology, vote Democrat.**

- **If you love having Radical Islamists as your elected representatives, vote Democrat.**

- **If Black and Brown people should just kill White people instead of ignoring them and go about their business, vote Democrat.**

- **If you want to give up your heating and air-conditioning to save the environment, vote Democrat. You won't.**

- **If honest debate is micro-aggression, vote Democrat.**

- **Since you probably don't realize Global Warming has been completely politicized, vote Democrat.**

- **Listen up GenX/Millennials: If you're traveling to Global Warming conferences in a private jet, yacht, or 10000 lb. armored vehicle, vote Democrat. Apparently, leading by example is inconvenient but at least it proves Global Warming is a hoax. Hollywood Hypocrisy should no longer be tolerated.**

- **To GenX/Millennials: If you want to be the first generation to do worse than your parents, vote Democrat.**

- **If you don't understand childbearing and overtime are responsible for the entire gender pay-gap, vote Democrat.**

• If you feel compelled to provide free health care to all Illegal Aliens, vote Democrat, but why stop there? Free food, Free booze..... You get my point.

• If Veterans should be abused, vote Democrat.

• If you want to die in a plane crash, vote Democrat. Terrorists are afraid of Trump.

• If GenX/Millennial and want your white-collar job outsourced, vote Democrat.

• If censorship should only apply to Conservatives, vote Democrat.

• If you want America to resemble a Sit-Com, vote Democrat.

• If you support the "Occupy" movement, vote
Democrat, then "Occupy" another country 'cause you
don't appreciate whatchagotricheer.

• If segregation interests you, vote Democrat because
Universities now segregate housing, graduation
ceremonies, and student orientation. I know. I couldn't
believe it either.

• If you prefer elected officials be politically correct
rather than honest, vote Democrat.

• If hearing women brag about their last abortion
animates you, vote Democrat.

- If you sleep on white sheets, vote Democrat 'cause that's what the KKK wears and white sheets are racist.

- If you find Democrat officials trustworthy, vote Democrat. What?

- If hurling stuff at cops makes you safe, vote Democrat.

- If Black and Hispanic media personalities, who each make over a million dollars a year, can possibly be your true voice or represent your life experience, vote Democrat.

- If you forget America is "Of, By, and For The People", vote Democrat.

• If you believe environmentalism is about the environment, vote Democrat. It's not. It's all politics.

• Looks like Hollywood has begun to encourage the Left to arm itself against the Right. If that sounds like a great idea, vote Democrat.

• If we should spend billions on Infrastructure, vote Democrat, but after taxing everyone to death, no one will have any money to use the wonderful infrastructure you just built.

• For Death Panels, vote Democrat.

• If you belong to a Teachers' Union in a leadership position you are a Communist, so you might as well vote Democrat. Same party.

- If Retard Porn is your thing, vote Democrat, then turn on 'The View'.

- If Female sports figures should make the same as Men though nobody watches them 'cause they're pretty boring, vote Democrat.

- If your place of Worship is now an Illegal Alien Bed'nBreakfast, vote Democrat.

- Since White Nationalists are responsible for all minority homicides in America, vote Democrat.

- If you hate thy neighbor, vote Democrat.

• If we should let everybody out of prison, vote Democrat.

• If you've slept your way to the top like Hollywood celebrities, vote Democrat.

• Listen very carefully GenX/Millennials: If placing different skin colors on robots to improve acceptance doesn't prove Tribalism is hardwired, vote Democrat. Hard racism in America no longer exists to any measurable degree. Tribalism? Otherism? Definitely. And we need to work on that! But it's been hardwired into the animal kingdom for millions of years as an innate protective mechanism so it's not going away anytime soon no matter what your skin color.

- If Trump is a dictator, vote Democrat, then learn about real dictators.

- If you are a Pedophile, vote Democrat.

- If you still think Trump is a Russian agent, vote Democrat. Seriously?

- If you can't understand that sanctuary for Illegal Aliens is a loss of sanctuary for everyone else, vote Democrat.

- If the B.E.T. isn't racist, vote Democrat.

- If you love China, vote Democrat, then move there, just remember to bring a shipping container full of gas masks 'cause nobody can breathe over there.

- If we should eliminate the concept of citizenship, vote Democrat.

- If you know what 'Progressive' means, vote Democrat. You don't. Nobody does.

- Listen up GenX/Millennials: Search for present-day pictures of Venezuela, if not impressed, vote Democrat. Then move there so you can bask in the warm sunshine of Democratic Socialism. Bring Bernie, every other Democratic Presidential candidate and the Squad with you.

- If Yoga and Meditation should replace contact sports and Military Exercise, vote Democrat.

- If you think Trump built cages in which to put kids, vote Democrat. Obama did. And they're not cages anyway, they were put up to protect kids from predators.

- If all your hard-earned savings evaporate because of profligate Washington spending, vote Democrat. Trump will get spending under control his second term.

- If you wanted to join ISIS but didn't get the chance before Trump wiped 'em out, vote Democrat.

- If neither curious nor inquisitive, vote Democrat.

● If it's hotter than usual in one part of the country, vote Democrat, but if you look carefully it's colder than usual in another. That is not Global Warming. It's the weather!


● If it's only fair Hollywood shares its fabulous wealth with poor people, vote Democrat. "Occupy Hollywood".


● If Economics is a subject that escapes you, vote Democrat.


● If reparations are in order, vote Democrat, but you must seize assets from descendants of Blacks and Indians who owned Black slaves. Let's start with Casinos and see what happens.

- If you walk around waiting to be offended, vote Democrat.

- If you can explain why an American with one drop of Black blood is Black, vote Democrat. I've never understood that.

- If any quota system seems non-discriminatory, vote Democrat.

- If unable to see that Trump manipulates the media like a bunch of trained seals, vote Democrat. Feel familiar?

- If watching the Democrat primary debates while sober, vote Democrat.

• If 9/11 should be celebrated, vote Democrat.

• If the word "owner" offends you, vote Democrat,
then give me all your s**t so you're no longer
burdened.

• If you want to work 'till you drop dead, vote
Democrat.

• Since you don't believe in marriage, vote Democrat.
Your kids will thank you.

• If Bureaucrats ever create anything, solve anything
or work in earnest for the citizenry, vote Democrat.

• If Hollywood is the Heartland, vote Democrat. Wow,
are you lost.

- If insecure in your home, vote Democrat. Then buy a shotgun.

- If seeing Poor White people makes you happy, vote Democrat.

- To GenX/Millennials: If you have no time for procreation, vote Democrat. That way everything can be about YOU.

- If our Military should be more compassionate, vote Democrat. Apparently, Australia just implemented such a policy. Let's follow that along and see how that works out. Bets anyone?

● If life is just so unfair, vote Democrat. It is. Get over it.


● If stupidity and dementia qualify you to be President, vote Democrat.


● If Ebola seems like a nice change of pace, vote Democrat.


● To GenX/Millennials: Since you haven't traveled to other countries much, vote Democrat, then get out more and see what a mess most countries are in.


● If Guantanamo should be emptied and inmates moved to your hometown, vote Democrat.

• If the Nigerian Mafia should be imported to America to help develop their business model, vote Democrat. I hear Shark Tank is interested.

• If not familiar with the concept of 'projection', vote Democrat. Look it up 'cause that's how this party's been operating for a while.

• If you think CO2 is a major greenhouse gas, vote Democrat. It's not. It's water vapor.

• If freedom scares you, vote Democrat, but unbridled government power should scare you a lot more.

• If Jeffrey Epstein is somebody with whom you'd like to associate, vote Democrat. He could really use a friend right about now.

• Listen carefully GenX/Millennials: If you forget "Equality" does not exist in nature, vote Democrat. When you hear "Level the Playing Field" or "Equality", it's BS. It exists only in Math.

• If restricting concealed carry makes sense, vote Democrat, but it's exactly the unknown carrier who keeps you safe and armed criminals guessing.

• To GenX/Millennials: If being judged is unfair, vote Democrat, but it's how we survive as a species.

• If the English language is no longer useful, vote Democrat.

- If sex slavery seems like a good business to be in, vote Democrat.

- If Comrade is your favorite pronoun, vote Democrat. Not zed?

- If you support rape, arson, and murder, vote Democrat. Fewer people. Good for the environment!

- If female, raped, but wait 100 years to report it, vote Democrat.

- If 'appeasement' is how you resolve most situations, vote Democrat.

- If George Washington University should be renamed "America Sucks and Needs to Die University", vote Democrat.

- If offended by 'all lives matter', vote Democrat. How 'bout "No lives matter'? Feel better now?

- If a Presidential candidate claims to be African American but is Indian, and you're seriously OK with that, vote Democrat. Talk about Cultural Appropriation.

- If electric bills should equal mortgage payments, vote Democrat.

- If governed by emotion instead of reason, vote Democrat.

- If you start every day looking for free stuff, vote Democrat.

- If Trump is a pompous ass, vote Democrat, then take a close look at your Democrat Representatives. Surprise!

- To GenX/Millennials: If you don't recognize most countries want America to fail and you to disappear, vote Democrat.

- If violent domestic riots around the globe are riveting, vote Democrat, 'cause you're next.

- If you want an insecure lunatic as President, vote Democrat.

• If our national anthem should be "God Damn America", vote Democrat. The Obama's prefer that version.

• Listen up GenX/Millennials: If desperate to lower CO2 levels, vote Democrat, however, CO2 levels have been off the charts while our planet was literally covered in ice. Please explain why you want to lower CO2 again?

• If gratitude has no place in modern society, vote Democrat.

• If bathing in the Washington swamp, vote Democrat, then shower in BleachBit. Hilary did.

• **If Concentration Camps in America exist, vote Democrat, but be careful not to get too close to the ovens or gas chambers.**

• **If knowing every locality managed by Democrats is a failure, vote Democrat, then move there.**

• **If price gouging by our Elite Universities doesn't anger you, vote Democrat. Oh yeah, Democrat policy produced that.**

• **If AOC doesn't offend you, vote Democrat, but you're pretty much alone.**

• **If you work hard, come home and can't wait to have your paycheck confiscated, vote Democrat.**

- If "Ignorance is bliss", vote Democrat.

- Since Trump will stay in the White House even after he loses, vote Democrat. Poor guy has nothin' to do. Maybe he'll open up a bunch of Hair Salons with Boris Johnson.

- If you studied White Supremacy, vote Democrat, but you're probably a racist. Just admit it. Feel better now?

- If China has our best interests at heart, vote Democrat.

- If America deserves to be a Third World Country, vote Democrat.

- If an immigrant and don't love the freedom and opportunity this country offers, vote Democrat, then pack your bags and get back to your S***thole.

- If your State has the highest number of Psychopaths, vote Democrat. I'm talking to you NY, NJ, Calif., Conn., Maine, Mass., Delaware, and Maryland. See a pattern here?

- If every White person is a White Supremacist, vote Democrat.

- If human waste and garbage on the streets somehow make you healthier, vote Democrat. I know, Bubonic Plague is so awesome, right?

● **Listen carefully GenX/Millennials: If you deny FB, Google, Twitter, the NYT, and Wash. Post are all products of White Privilege, vote Democrat, but in shutting them down you'd be recognizing our racist past. How 'bout it?**

● **If over 40, vote Democrat, but think about a brain transplant.**

● **If able to trace your American heritage back 9 or 10 generations, vote Democrat, but your ancestors probably owned slaves.**

● **If you apologize for being born, vote Democrat, and don't forget to remind your kids and grandkids to do the same.**

• If you need to be liked more than respected, vote Democrat.

• If comfortable with most individuals within the Obama administration being corrupt, vote Democrat. They belong in prison. The good news; you can probably vote for them while there.

• If a Climate Expert, vote Democrat. You're not and if you say you are you're probably a political hack. Bill Nye what? What a douche.

• If elected officials should spend at least 100 years in office, vote Democrat.

• If taking care of yourself is inconvenient, vote Democrat. Don't worry, the Government will always have your back. 'Ya.

• If Black and Hispanic Studies majors come out fair-minded, vote Democrat.

• If 'Hail Satan' should start and end all invocations, vote Democrat.

• If you find everyone 'whitesplaining', vote Democrat but you are probably a racist.

• If you want forced organ harvesting, vote Democrat. Communists do, and your party's ethos is pretty much the same.

• Blind to the fact that every Democrat Presidential Candidate has accomplished almost nothing during their lifetime, vote Democrat.

• If American flags should be burned instead of displayed, vote Democrat.

• If backing reparations, vote Democrat, but you must give them to descendants of poor whites who couldn't afford slaves.

• If no higher power exists, vote Democrat, but Who or What created the Universe?

• If meaningful problem-solving legislation is obsolete, vote Democrat.

• Listen carefully GenX/Millennials: If a debt
>$1,000,000 for every US citizen doesn't scare the crap
out of you (Green New Deal and Medicare For All),
vote Democrat. That's a hole from which you'll never
escape. Now; if you re-elect Trump he may restructure
the debt during his second term.

• If our Southern Border should be renamed 'North
Mexico', vote Democrat.

• If you feel sorry for present-day American Indians,
vote Democrat, but bear in mind they fought with the
British and French against us.

• If a rabid anti-semite, vote Democrat.

- **Listen up GenX/Millennials: If we should be more like Sweden, vote Democrat but their society and culture are disintegrating because of forced immigration.**

- **If rich people should leave America, vote Democrat. Then see what happened in Turkey, India, Brazil, France, and China.**

- **If The Muslim Brotherhood interests you, vote Democrat.**

- **If not understanding jobs in America are color blind, vote Democrat. Admittedly, institutional racism was part of our culture years ago.**

- **Listen up GenX/Millennials: If truth and freedom aren't important anymore, vote Democrat. It was before the Internet and Social Media really screwed things up.**

- **If you enjoy the sound of morning prayer coming from Minarets, vote Democrat.**

- **If Gay or Trans soldiers are better than Cis-gender, vote Democrat.**

- **If staff abuse by Democrat candidates is acceptable, vote Democrat.**

- **If Drug Price disclosure to the public makes you uncomfortable, vote Democrat. Trump's working on that.**

- If a guy named Colon should decide what shoes you wear, vote Democrat. Please consider calling for advice on hair styling as well.

- If not incredibly obvious legal immigrants tend to assimilate and illegals don't, vote Democrat.

- If disarmament is empowering, vote Democrat.

- If you start virtue-signaling before your morning coffee, vote Democrat.

- If State and Local taxes should just keep going up, vote Democrat.

- If working in a Government sweatshop has been a life-long dream, vote Democrat. Sorry Postal Workers.

- If offshore wind farms should be constructed, vote Democrat, then say goodbye to fresh fish forever.

- If good intentions are better than good results, vote Democrat.

- If socially engineered, vote Democrat.

- If Cartels, Angry Mobs, Roving Gangs, and Sleeper Cells are things this country could use a bit more of, vote Democrat.

- To GenX/Millennials: If America's standard of living is a total embarrassment, vote Democrat.

- If you want to live in constant fear, vote Democrat.

- If Obama is God, vote Democrat.

- Supporting reparations, vote Democrat, but just remember the North benefited from slavery almost as much as the South.

- If Tampon dispensers in Men's Rooms should be mandatory, vote Democrat.

- If sucking up is what you do best, vote Democrat.

- If MAGA hats scare you, vote Democrat. They should.

- If the American flag should be replaced by the Rainbow Flag, vote Democrat. It is way prettier.

- If man-made Global Warming is real(it's not), vote Democrat, just remember warmer->more clouds->cooling so the whole process is self-correcting.

- If Poverty for All, Prosperity for None should be featured on all Democrat publications, vote Democrat.

- If feeling like a foreigner in your own country just feels 'right', vote Democrat.

- Refusing to vaccinate your kids, vote Democrat; we need fewer of you.

- If you support the Status Quo, vote Democrat.

• If looking forward every morning to reading about women and children killed by Illegal Aliens, vote Democrat.

• If laws don't matter, vote Democrat.

• Listen up GenX/Millennials: If OK with most Politicians owing their entire careers to other Politicians, vote Democrat.

• If unable to judge the quality of data, vote Democrat, then learn critical thinking.

• If belonging to a thoroughly corrupt Government Union in any way improves your life, vote Democrat.

- If our Constitution was written exclusively by racists, vote Democrat, but why does the Declaration of Independence unequivocally claim "all men are created equal"?

- If getting brainwashed and propagandized is among your favorite activities, vote Democrat.

- If a Liberal Arts Major, vote Democrat because you can't think for yourself and you're probably a Communist. Well, ok, a Fascist.

- Listen up GenX/Millennials: If your news comes from Facebook or Twitter, vote Democrat, then consider subscribing to Pravda or Al Jazeera.

- If a slave to the Democrat party, vote Democrat, then demand reparations.

- To GenX/Millennials: If the climate changes as frequently as your underwear, vote Democrat.

- Forgetting YOU are the Government, vote Democrat.

- If you just can't wait for the next Christian genocide, vote Democrat.

- If Socialist or Communist, vote Democrat; both are forms of Slavery but don't expect reparations any time soon.

• If LGBTQ, vote Democrat, then see how you're treated elsewhere. Try the Middle East, China, Chechnya, Russia….. You get the point.

• To GenX/Millennials: Never hearing of the "Quaternary Glaciation", vote Democrat, then look it up. Hint: We are in a minor ice age right now! Hint: Melting ice is a good thing. Hint: Expect more of it and adapt. Hint: Adaptation is what humans do best.

• If elected officials should live like Kings and Queens, vote Democrat.

• If embarrassed to admit you are attracted to the opposite sex, vote Democrat.

• If every other country produces higher quality goods than America, vote Democrat, then look at the returns counter in Customer Service at Walmart.

• If a Holocaust Denier, vote Democrat. The KKK needs more people like you.

• If consistently wrong on Policy decisions, vote Democrat.

• If you've had more Plastic Surgery than years in Congress, vote Democrat.

• If Blacks should be replaced by Hispanics, vote Democrat.

- If you hate the way Trump speaks, vote Democrat, then listen to other New Yorkers from Queens.

- If a snowflake, vote Democrat.

- If " One Nation, Under God, Indivisible, with Liberty and Justice for all" is racist, vote Democrat.

- If Liberalism is 'settled science', vote Democrat.

- If all American businesses should be State-owned, vote Democrat.

- If morally superior, obnoxious and self-aggrandizing, vote Democrat.

• If America deserves getting its ass kicked by other countries, vote Democrat.

• If unable to differentiate hard racism from the soft racism of low expectations, vote Democrat.

• If Mike Pence is pure evil, vote Democrat. Have you seen this guy? Evil?

• If Americans are the dumbest, fattest laziest people on Earth, vote Democrat, then look in the mirror.

• If LA RAZA is not a Hispanic Supremacy Group, vote Democrat.

• If anything in the Mainstream Media seems real, vote Democrat.

• **Listen up GenX/Millennials: If you simply forgot Sea Levels go DOWN if the Arctic Ice Cap MELTS, vote Democrat. Place water and ice cubes in a glass and watch them melt. The water level goes DOWN, as would sea levels if the Arctic Ice Cap melts.**

• **If Medicaid is great health insurance, vote Democrat.**

• **If you like Netflix's "Dear White People", vote Democrat, 'cause "blacksplaining" will surely bring us all together.**

• **If America needs more Fentanyl, vote Democrat.**

• **If Government Housing is the best place to live, vote Democrat.**

• **If Sharia law is preferable to Judeo-Christian principles, vote Democrat. I hear Iran is nice this time of year and you're just in time for their 'Gay Pride Parade'.**

• **If statues scare you, vote Democrat.**

• **Since Black and Brown people never blurt out, Honkey, Cracker, Whitey, Hillbilly, Peckerhead, Redneck, or Trailer Trash, vote Democrat, because "people of color" can't be racist.**

• **If you prefer to raise your kids in poverty, vote Democrat.**

- If America should rely primarily on other countries for our energy and natural resources, vote Democrat.

- If civility has no place in civil society, vote Democrat.

- If a member of the Communist party #RedforEd movement, vote Democrat.

- If complaining is what you do best, vote Democrat.

- If you find Rapinoe or O'Donnell the least bit likable, vote Democrat.

- If everything is relative, vote Democrat.

- If the Feds should be in charge of all education in America, vote Democrat.

- If Presidential personality is more important than Presidential policy, vote Democrat.

- If reciting the Pledge of Allegiance is obsolete, vote Democrat.

- If 100% of Americans are gay or should be, vote Democrat.

- If you still live in your parents' basement, vote Democrat, and stock up on Red Bull and Doritos cause you're gonna be there awhile.

- If you believe in killing cops, vote Democrat.

• If cow farts are an existential threat, vote Democrat, then hang out in elevators awhile.

• Listen up GenX/Millennials: If foreign unskilled labor will be needed in the age of robotics and AI, vote Democrat. It won't. And you want to remove our Southern Border Wall?

• If you have an overwhelming desire to donate all of your assets to the government, vote Democrat. Republicans already do.

• Forgetting all Black Congressmen use to be Republican, vote Democrat.

• To GenX/Millennials: If you no longer want to burn fossil fuels and WALK everywhere (especially to

Hawaii and Puerto Rico), vote Democrat. Maybe Colon can get you some of those Betsy Ross sneakers and attach some floaties?

• If men are better equipped emotionally and physically to bear and raise children, vote Democrat.

• If Jewish, vote Democrat, but you just voted for the first party to come right out and say they hate Jews.

• If taking a close look at Democrat Representatives and Senators does not yield major disappointment, vote Democrat. And BTW, same for many Republican too.

• If females should be replaced by transgenders in all sports, vote Democrat.

- If utopian visions dominate your life, vote Democrat.

- If America is more corrupt, violent, and unjust than most other countries, vote Democrat.

- If all women are better off without men, vote Democrat. Some? Yes!

- If Jussie Smollet is innocent, vote Democrat. So's Madoff and OJ.

- To GenX/Millennials: If Margaret Sanger should be praised for starting Planned Parenthood, vote Democrat, but remember, she called it "The Negro Project" to promote racial cleansing.

• **If the Middle Class is thriving under Liberalism, vote Democrat.**

• **If you understand what Social Justice means, vote Democrat. You don't. Nobody does. It's a totally meaningless term like Climate Change.**

• **If looking at Hilary Clinton does not make you breathe a deep sigh of relief, vote Democrat.**

• **If gay and transgender people have fewer 'issues' than most, vote Democrat.**

• **If C.A.I.R. is not a Muslim Supremacy Group, vote Democrat.**

• If the US Government should print unlimited quantities of money to fund the Green New Deal and Medicare for all, vote Democrat. At least you won't need to buy toilet paper anymore.

• If abolishing Columbus Day turns you on, vote Democrat, then go back to work 'cause you don't deserve the day off.

• If inner-city Chicago and Baltimore should be role models for the rest of the country, vote Democrat.

• Listen up GenX/Millennials: If you believe nuclear energy is too dangerous, vote Democrat then do some reading about 4th Generation reactors. Nuclear Energy is the only reliable 'Green' source of limitless energy. If the wind blew and the sun shone continuously it would be a different story.

• If you hate everyone who doesn't look like you, vote Democrat.

• If all Churches across America should be burned to the ground, vote Democrat.

• If National Socialist Democrats like AOC or Bernie are heroes, vote Democrat. (The National Socialist Party was the Nazi Party). Look it up.

• Listen up GenX/Millennials: If you don't understand Solar activity and Milankovitch Cycles determine climate, vote Democrat. It's not CO2.

- **If Social Media is unbiased, vote Democrat.**

- **If you'd like to hear "Allahu Akbar" at the beginning of sporting events, political speeches, and public school, vote Democrat.**

- **If reparations are in order, vote Democrat, but make damn sure to include the families of the 340,000 Northern white boys who died in the Civil War.**

- **If High-Speed Rail or Hyperloop will be affordable transportation, vote Democrat, but we can't afford to build 'em much less ride 'em.**

- **If Jews are the 'real problem', vote Democrat.**

- If America's poorest are worse off than other countries, vote Democrat.

- If standards should be abolished, vote Democrat.

- If heroin, meth, crack, Ecstasy, and Fentanyl should all be legalized and freely available to all, vote Democrat.

- If your Government should be controlled by Corporations, vote Democrat. Oh wait, they are.

- To GenX/Millennials: If you honestly believe other countries will stop dumping Carbon into the atmosphere, vote Democrat. They won't. Why? Most other countries know "Man-Made" Global Warming is BS.

- If we should no longer teach American history, vote Democrat.

- If able to watch CNN, MSNBC, ABC, CBS, NPR or NBC without becoming enraged, vote Democrat.

- If rugged individualism scares you, vote Democrat. It should.

- If David Duke is your hero, vote Democrat because the KKK is a Democrat institution. Always has been.

- Since Democratic National Socialism has done wonders for the USSR, Nazi Germany, Cuba and Venezuela, vote Democrat.

• If America needs more Tuberculosis, Measles, Mumps, Whooping Cough, HIV, Rabies, Hepatitis A, Influenza, and Syphilis, vote Democrat.

• If you hate all European Christians because they founded this country, vote Democrat.

• If "Made in America" embarrasses you, vote Democrat.

• If America should have a One Party system, vote Democrat. The "Legalize Marijuana Now Party" and "The Rent is Too Damn High Party" seem kinda fun.

• If Public Schools are well run, have high standards, and promote disciplined learning, vote Democrat.

- If America should beg forgiveness from other countries, vote Democrat.

- If anger is your prime motivation, vote Democrat.

- If your brain can only be found on colonoscopy, vote Democrat.

- If we should outsource our Military, vote Democrat.

- If Mainstream Media is honest, trustworthy, fair, objective and impartial, vote Democrat.

- If Conservative thought should be considered immoral, vote Democrat.

• If Female Genital Mutilation is a force for good, vote Democrat.

• If color counts more than character, vote Democrat.

• If Cities and States with the highest taxes are the very best places to live, vote Democrat.

• If migrant women from Central America deserve to be raped, vote Democrat.

• If not thoroughly embarrassed by now for voting Democrat, vote Democrat, but you really should pay more attention to what others are saying and thinking about your voting habits.

• **If you vote Democrat and want to leave the country or watch cartoons on Election Day, it's OK.**

• **If you look forward to mass murder so Liberal agendas can be advanced, vote Democrat.**

• **If a Climate Alarmist, hysterical about yearly routine Summer glacial ice melt, vote Democrat.**

• **If wanting to see more gun violence from Hollywood, vote Democrat, but when Hollywood calls for more gun control let them know that they need to stop producing massive full-feature non-stop gun violence before we can take them seriously.**

• Believing Trump is personally responsible for everything from genocide to bad breath, vote Democrat.

• Understanding that there is no reason for a White person to be in the Democrat party, vote Democrat so they can be deleted from voter rolls.

• If nobody feels comfortable around you because of your personality, vote Democrat.

• If concerned as to why White Extremists are enraged, vote Democrat, though nobody questions other groups' motivations. Ever.

• With illegal immigration, Emergency Room mortality rates are up over 50% so if you get your care at your local ER, vote Democrat.

• If you killed Jeffrey Epstein, vote Democrat.

• "Those who do not learn history are doomed to repeat it", so vote Democrat because you guys don't learn anything anyway.

• If practicing Schadenfreude, vote Democrat because if you get power again you'll have plenty to go around.

• Tree-lined streets are known to bring happiness and health to all, so vote Democrat if you want to lower CO2 and kill all the trees and make everyone sick and depressed.

• If you want to live in a shipping container, vote Democrat.

• Since White people take up too much space in College, vote Democrat so they can be immediately removed.

• If reading seems like too much work, vote Democrat.

• If all Democrats should be given free semi-automatic weapons to hunt Conservatives, vote Democrat. You're thinking about it, aren't cha?

• If a full-blown recession is something to be encouraged just to get Trump out, vote Democrat. You're gonna try though.

- If brain-dead drugged-out musicians are your best source of political information, vote Democrat.

- If the name "Castro" seems like a good name for a Democrat, vote Democrat because the Castro's are pretty much all the same both here and in Cuba.

- If Hollywood virtue signaling doesn't make you want to stop watching anything they produce, vote Democrat.

- Since Black Lives in Chicago Don't Matter, vote Democrat.

• If naive enough to believe Governments will allow Bitcoin to exist in order to bypass taxation, vote Democrat.

• If knife and fork control prevents obesity, vote Democrat.

• If Illegal Aliens should hunt American Citizens, vote Democrat.

• Since White people control Hollywood, and Hollywood hates White people, vote Democrat so we can get rid of all the White people in Hollywood.

• Since the Clintons arranged for Jeffery Epstein to be off Suicide Watch, vote Democrat to show your approval of Arkancide.

• Since cars and knives kill more people than guns, vote Democrat so we can begin Background Checks on all knife and car owners. And power tools too.

• If recycling makes you gay, vote Democrat. I tried it. It's true.

• If you can't see that the athletes who take a knee or pump a fist while our National Anthem plays are self-absorbed vainglorious narcissistic assholes, vote Democrat.

• If encouraging LGTBQ lifestyle should start aggressively in pre-school and increase exponentially K-12, vote Democrat.

• **If the Vatican should establish our immigration policy, vote Democrat.**

• **If sodomy and oral sex should be the only legally sanctioned forms of human sexual contact, vote Democrat.**

• **If Govt. investigations should last forever, cost billions of dollars and never find anything, vote Democrat. Oh wait, they do.**

• **If you haven't paid taxes your entire life and want even more stuff from the Gov't, vote Democrat.**

• **If here illegally, killing citizens, but demanding your 'civil rights' once caught, vote Democrat.**

• If it's a great idea for 4-year-olds to 'come out of the closet' and reveal they're gay, bi, or whatever, vote Democrat. Just out of diapers with no hormones to speak of. Yes, Them. And you think Global Warming is an existential threat?

• If New Jersey Muslims should slash tires of cars owned by Jews, vote Democrat.

• If Sadiq Khan should be the next Mayor of NY, vote Democrat.

• If American Muslims should be butchering animals in their back-yards, vote Democrat.

• **If our Govt. couldn't keep Jeffrey Epstein alive but you believe they can somehow keep sick people alive, vote Democrat.**

• **If every white candidate running for President should be replaced by a "Candidate of Color", vote Democrat.**

• **Now that Trump is trying to buy Greenland, vote Democrat so all Conservatives can move there while you die of Global Warming.**

• **Whereas Russia, Global Warming and Racism are all hoaxes, vote Democrat so we can keep these going even longer and regain the House.**

- **Loving Obama, vote Democrat, but if he wasn't a Racist, why did he surround himself with Black advisors?**

- **Believing Global Warming is real, vote Democrat then set your thermostat to 105 degrees in summer and 5 degrees in winter.**

- **To GenX/Z/Millennials: If you have no idea what freedom actually means, vote Democrat. Look it up because if you vote Democrat you can kiss it goodbye.**

- **Living in a city and seeing most crosswalk figures are White, vote Democrat so we can change them to Black, Brown or Rainbow.**

• If Micheal Brown was murdered(hands up don't shoot), vote Democrat but not a single piece of evidence points in that direction. Not one.

• If criticizing or poking fun is the same as the N-Word, vote Democrat so we can end all meaningful human communication.

• If lawns are Racist and should be destroyed and replaced by Brown, Red or Black dirt(kinda racist) vote Democrat. PS: Lawns inhale $CO_2$ and exhale $O_2$. Yeah, let's get rid of 'em.

• If all sexual allegations should be 'guilty until proven innocent', vote Democrat but you must also agree that in the future there will be no sexual contact whatsoever without a lawyer present.

- If there is life outside our solar system, vote Democrat but you'll never see it because they self-destruct as a consequence of Liberalism.

- If voter suppression exists, vote Democrat because Democrats believe Black and Hispanic people aren't smart enough to get ID cards.

- If you forget that Humanity flourishes during warming periods and dies off during ice ages, vote Democrat. During the last ice age humanity almost went extinct.

- If you're too dense to recognize men weaponize their strength and women weaponize their beauty, vote Democrat.

•A.O.C. wants to have 'one less child' due to Global Warming so vote Democrat if you think she should have no kids, since who wants to see her kids burst into flames when the Earth warms to the surface temperature of the Sun?

• If selfish enough to ignore your biological imperative to procreate, vote Democrat.

• If we should replace green cards with Marijuana cards, get illegal aliens totally baked and deport them before they realize it, vote Democrat.

• If no longer believing is heterosexuality, vote Democrat, but you will be destroying the American population, your family and heirs.

• If wanting to cure Cancer, vote Democrat, but understand there isn't enough money to fight both Global Warming and cure Cancer at the same time. PS: Cancer is not a hoax.

• If you reside here and want to speak a foreign language in public, vote Democrat. But here's what pisses off Americans: If you're a tourist, speak whatever you want. If a RESIDENT, speak English in public and whatever you want at home. Why? Because if you don't want to speak our language in public you don't respect our culture and you don't want to assimilate. Guests respect their hosts.

Slight change in format but the content is still vituperative!

- If transgender fashion models should replace all cis-gender just to 'even the playing field' and eliminate sexism in the industry, vote Democrat.

- Since the Electoral College is affirmative action for White people, vote Democrat, but you must also acknowledge kindergarten is affirmative action for the Squad.

- Listen up GenZ/X/Millennials: If being born on top of the food chain isn't enough for you, vote Democrat.

- Hating Jeffrey Epstein, vote Democrat so that when you learn of any Hollywood celebrity who partied with him you can be sure to boycott anything they do in the future. Betchwon't.

- **Whereas the Democrats are the only party that will protect you, vote Democrat but be aware you'll be long dead before they show up.**

- **If plagued by Gender issues, vote Democrat and consider getting help as recent studies suggest that many of you are not well.**

- **Plants are now known to have feelings just like humans so if you want to lower CO2 and suffocate them to death, vote Democrat.**

- **Biodiversity being paramount, vote Democrat since there are way too many humans competing with other species and it only seems fair to remove yourselves from the equation.**

- **Since you will never be happy again no matter what happens to you, vote Democrat.**

- **In DeBlasio's NY there is apparently no difference between geniuses and morons so vote Democrat to prevent future Smartism.**

- **If Black colleges are not fundamentally Racist, vote Democrat.**

- **If fluent in Mandarin, vote Democrat 'cause if you get the White House you're gonna need it.**

- **Listen up GenZ/X/Millennials: Looks like cell phones are emitting all sorts of radiation and frying your brains, therefore, vote Democrat so** we can identify you. You'll be the ones with smoking ears and a blank stare.

- **Whereas cows now wear fart-o-meters, vote Democrat, so we can get as many Democrats as possible to wear them which seems only fair since you guys are the ones screaming about Global Warming.**

- **Seeing as gun manufacturers produce guns that produce bigotry and hate, vote Democrat so we can make guns out of cotton candy and rainbows. People too.**

- **Proving Global Warming is a hoax considering the Obama's just bought a beachfront mansion,** vote Democrat 'cause you will always praise him

no matter what he does.


- **Boycott is a sexist term and needs to be replaced by Girlcott, Transcott, Bicott or Gaycott so vote Democrat because words have meaning especially hate-filled sexist words like boycott.**


- **Every time you listen to a Democrat politician you get dumber so if you've been listening quite a while, vote Democrat.**


- **To GenZ/X/Millennials: You live in one of the cleanest countries on Earth and don't know it, so vote Democrat if you must but take a good look at the environment of other countries before you** go all "America Sucks" and "Existential Threat" on us.

- If you want to prove to the world that you learned absolutely nothing in school, vote Democrat.

- If feeling the need to sign in to FB every morning to see what you should have for breakfast, vote Democrat.

- Until such time as girls are responsible for asking guys to marry them, vote Democrat and don't say a thing about inequality until then.

- If you actually know what's in a 'chicken nugget' vote Democrat because all your whining has now created meatless chicken nuggets so now we know even less about the crap we're shoving in our faces.

- Knowing we need way more anchor babies, vote Democrat so we can tattoo tiny anchors on all Black and White babies so Hispanic babies don't feel discriminated against.

- If hearing more from Hillary Clinton thrills you, vote Democrat.

- If having Ivy League college classrooms exclusively for Black only, White only and Hispanic only is 'Progressive', vote Democrat.

- **Hamas has been sending massive rockets into Israeli music concerts to kill as many civilian kids as possible and seeing as Democrats hate Jews, vote Democrat to show your support.**

- **If believing you know the first thing about Donald Trump, vote Democrat which proves you don't.**

- **Having recently lost your sense of humor and no longer able to laugh or smile, vote Democrat.**

- **Whereas men and women are exactly the same, vote Democrat so we can observe females playing in the NFL with 350 lb. defensive linemen turning them into pancakes.**

- Global Warming is already here and you're all going to die shortly so why vote Democrat? Republicans may vote 'cause they don't believe it.

- If you are concerned about Fires in the Amazon(not the Amazon Firestick which is different), vote Democrat, but the release of CO2 from those fires will make the Earth even greener than it is today.

- If you like the concept of crossing the Atlantic on a Zero-Carbon Yacht, vote Democrat but flying your entire team across the Atlantic makes complete fools out of both you and them.

- Since we're all 'gonna spontaneously combust by next Tuesday, vote Democrat so we can buy the Himalayan Mountains, move there, and start building 'Yak-fil-A' franchises.

- If the Ten Commandments seem a bit wordy, vote Democrat so we can consolidate them down to one, " Thou shalt now kill those who believe in Global Warming, everyone else, fuhgeddaboudit".

- Since every mascot is now considered racist, sexist, colonialist, activist, and capitalist, vote Democrat so we can remove anything that makes us happy.

- If having your children stabbed to death while walking their dog is not that big a deal, vote Democrat, if it is, re-elect Trump.

- Listen up GenZ/X/Millennials: If you forget the only 'existential threats' to your generation are supervolcanoes and meteors, vote Democrat. Any other time you hear that phrase, it's BS.

- If you have a fascination with retardation, vote Democrat.

- If being replaced by an avatar seems like the right approach to living a full life, vote Democrat since your party is in bed with Silicon Valley.

- **Believing in Global Warming, vote Democrat, but the only way to cool our planet(dumb idea) is to plant more trees and not try or talk about all the other crap you come up with.**

- **If the "Boy Scouts" should be renamed "Gender-neutral Non-binary, Non-judgemental Transitionally-fluid Scouts" vote Democrat.**

- **Since Measles is now in 30 States, vote Democrat so we can Nationalize it and get it to all 50 States by 2020.**

- **If unthinkable policy decisions should become routine, vote Democrat.**

- **Whereas sexual orientation has been proven to be genetic, vote Democrat so we can glorify LGBTQ status even more since it's 'not their fault'.**

- **If unable to see that even the weather has been politicized, vote Democrat.**

- **Whereas Islam is a 'Religion of Peace', vote Democrat so we can get adopt Sharia and become more peaceful like Europe and the Middle East as we ignore all the mistakes they've made regarding Immigration Policy.**

- **Listen up GenZ/X/Millennials: If wanting asylum seeking migrants to live a better life than you, vote Democrat.**

- **Since every single Democrat policy is hyperbolic stupid, vote Democrat and have every Policy backfire so we can regain the House and get a super-majority in the Senate.**

- **If "freedom's just another word for nothing left to lose", vote Democrat then give your freedom to a Conservative who actually appreciates it.**

- **Seeing as you love Chinese 'freedom' more than ours, vote Democrat, but take a look at Hong Kong where people are fighting to protect theirs.**

- **Listen up GenZ/X/Millennials: If you enjoy going out for any type of ethnic food, vote Democrat, but your 'cultural appropriation' is showing and**

you need to restrict your diet to burgers, BBQ,
twinkies and S'mores.

- **Whereas violence is Democrat policy ,vote
  Democrat so we can replace regular cocktails
  with Molotov cocktails.**

- **Looks like your party wants to cancel all student
  debt, credit card debt and healthcare debt so vote
  Democrat if collapsing our economy, promoting
  civil war and disintegrating your future seem
  prudent.**

- **Open-air urinals are not sexist and disgusting
  enough so vote Democrat and let's begin open-air**

commodes for both men and women in the name of equality and social justice.

- If  Liberal Supreme Court Justices should stay on the Bench at least 100 years after passing away, vote Democrat.

- If every single American business should be owned and operated by females, vote Democrat. Oh yeah, they should only employ women too.

- Considering Democrats are responsible for all recent mass shootings because they promote violence, vote Democrat so you can keep up the good work you've started.

- **If wanting to curb mass shootings, vote Democrat so we can promote mandatory conscription like Switzerland and Israel, aggressively vet all potential gun owners, keep an eye on them, update their training and keep them in the Reserves. And you want to take away guns? Nonsense.**

- **The Pope says Global Warming is an emergency but since you are undoubtedly a Church-going, devout Christian, vote Democrat so we can all go to Heaven where it's -454.81F. Bring a sweater.**

- **If you feel no shame in promoting violence, vote Democrat.**

- If we should only elect poverty-stricken people so they can get a taste of the good life, stay in office forever and steal us blind, vote Democrat.

- If all Journalism Schools should first teach their students how to lie, vote Democrat.

- If you know why recent hurricanes are not hitting the U.S., vote Democrat. I do. They're afraid of Trump.

- Since you're a Communist, vote Democrat, but businesses are leaving China in droves and either returning here or going to Non-Communist countries because Communism simply doesn't work. Period.

- As a Democrat you favor donkeys so vote Democrat if you want to bring your comfort donkey with you on all foreign and domestic flights.


- If the phrase 'if true' comes up a lot in your conversations, vote Democrat so we can pretty much dismiss anything we hear from you.


- If you're a victim, vote Democrat. But here's the truth. Minority status does not = Victim. Majority status does not = Predator. Democrat-inspired Paranoia and lack of historical perspective drives most people to the Democrat Party. I guarantee should you change party affiliation, your paranoia will

**immediately disappear because you will be part of the silent <u>Majority</u>. See how easy that was?**

- **If you've never heard of the Overton Window, vote Democrat. Overton what? It describes the way even the dumbest, radical, most mystifying Democrat policies can go from totally Unthinkable stupidity to actual policy by manipulation, obfuscation, lying, corruption and scandal (Think slavery reparations in Evanston Il). Only a Republican Congress and WH can prevent such madness. It is imperative we convince Democrats to stay home on Election Day and watch cartoons.**

- Just got back from a food court and was served some Asian food on a beautiful handcrafted bamboo disposable plate. Impressive. On top of that fancy plate was some of the worst crap I'd ever eaten. Tasteless, stale, and well past its prime. Then I thought I just sat through a perfect metaphor for the Democrat Party. See if you agree. If you don't, vote Democrat.